I READ! YOU READ!

Child's Turn to Read

Adult's Turn to Read

WE READ ABOUT

The Right to Vote

Tracy Vonder Brink and Madison Parker

Table of Contents

SEAHORSE PUBLISHING

Parent and Caregiver Guide

Reading aloud with your child has many benefits. It expands vocabulary, sparks discussion, and promotes an emotional bond. Research shows that children who have books read aloud to them have improved language skills, leading to greater school success.

I Read! You Read! books offer a fun and easy way to read with your child. Follow these guidelines.

Before Reading

- Look at the front and back covers. Discuss personal experiences that relate to the topic.
- Read the *Words to Know* at the back of the book. Talk about what the words mean.
- If the book will be challenging or unfamiliar to your child, read it aloud by yourself the first time. Then, invite your child to participate in a second reading.

During Reading

CHILD Have your child read the words beside this symbol. This text has been carefully matched to the reading and grade levels shown on the cover.

ADULT You read the words beside this symbol.

- Stop often to discuss what you are reading and to make sure your child understands.
- If your child struggles with decoding a word, help them sound it out. If it is still a challenge, say the word for your child and have them repeat it after you.
- To find the meaning of a word, look for clues in the surrounding words and pictures.

After Reading

- Praise your child's efforts. Notice how they have grown as a reader.
- Use the *Comprehension Questions* at the back of the book.
- Discuss what your child learned and what they liked or didn't like about the book.

Most importantly, let your child know that reading is fun and worthwhile. Keep reading together as your child's skills and confidence grow.

The Right to Vote

CHILD

The teacher says, "Let's **vote** on today's snack!"

The class chooses to have grapes.

You can **vote** for anything. Voting is a good way to settle a disagreement.

ADULT

Voting is how a group makes one **choice**.

People in the United States vote for who runs the country and more.

Each voter in the United States chooses the person they think would do the best job.

People vote for the **president** and CHILD
other leaders.

Not everyone can vote.

People also vote for the governor of their state, ADULT
the mayor of their city, and the people who will
represent them in the U.S. Congress.

People vote for the president every four years.

Voters must be at least 18 years old.

They must live where they vote.

They must be **citizens**.

The 26th Amendment to the U.S. Constitution lowered the voting age requirement from 21 to 18, so more young people could vote.

Voters learn about those who want to be leaders.

They think about who to choose.

CHILD

Voters research the candidates for each government job. They try to find out which one agrees most with their opinions.

ADULT

Voters want good leaders.

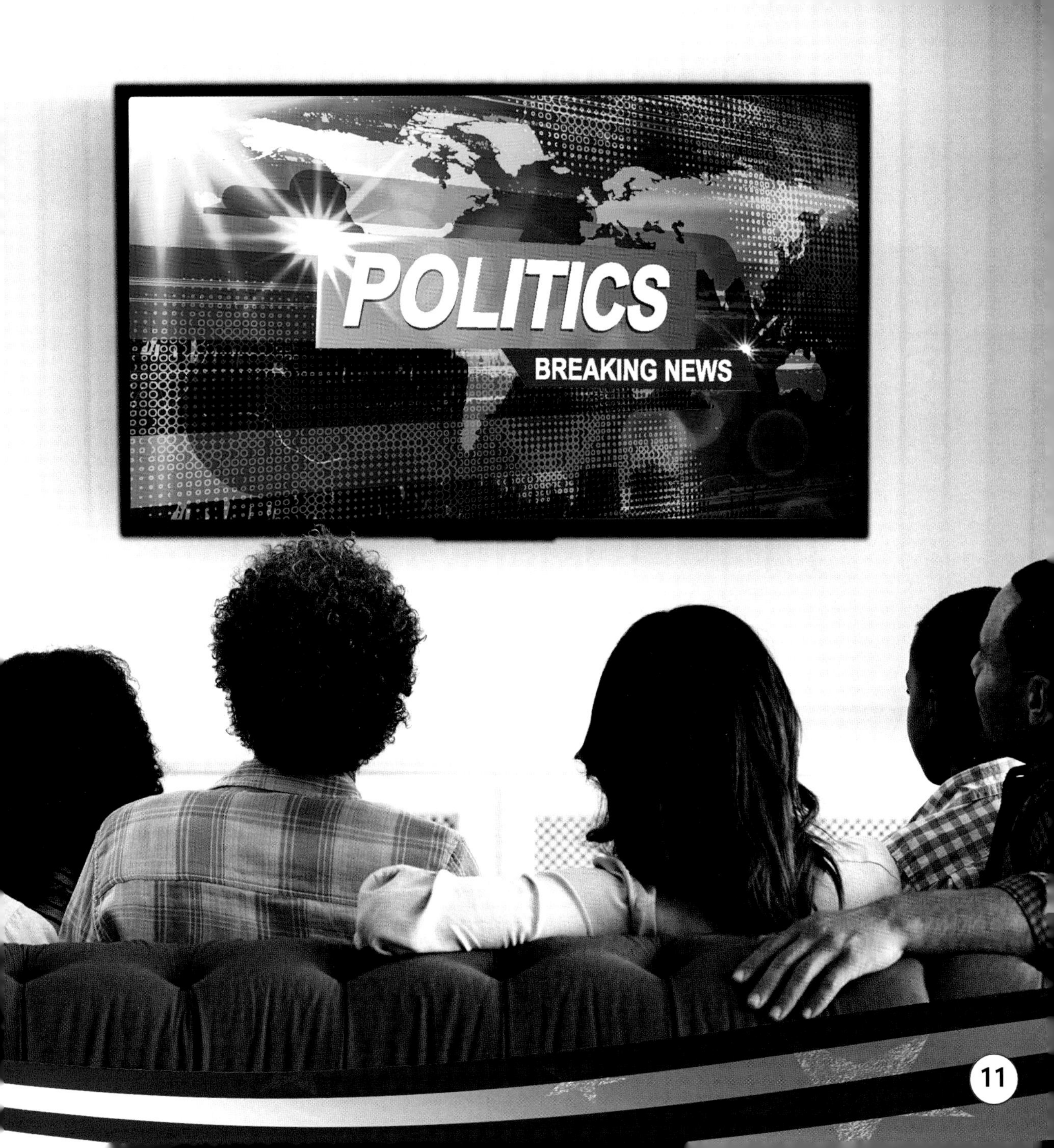
POLITICS
BREAKING NEWS

Election Day is the special day for voting.

CHILD

The **ballot** has the names of those who want to be leaders.

Voters mark the person they want.

In the U.S., Election Day is always on the Tuesday after the first Monday in November.

ADULT

Each person may mark only one ballot.

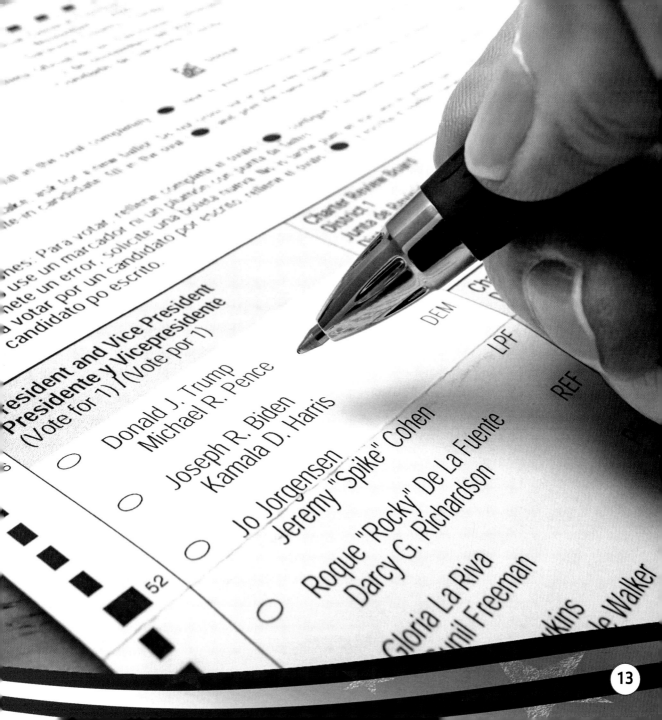

Some voters go to a **polling place**. CHILD

It may be a school. It may be a library.

Voters mark the ballot there.

Some states use paper **ballots** that get scanned by a computer. Other states have digital ballots. ADULT

Other voters stay home.

Their ballot comes in the mail.

The voter marks it and sends it back.

CHILD

This type of voting is called mail-in voting. People in the military who are overseas use mail-in ballots since they are unable to vote in person.

ADULT

Elections Official
123 Campaign Street
Township, State 45678

NO F
NEC
IF MA
POST

VOTE-BY-MAIL BALLO

BUSINESS RE

FIRST CLASS

All votes are counted.

The person with the most votes wins.

CHILD

Most votes are counted by a computer. If there is a question about a ballot, it gets reviewed by a special group of people.

ADULT

Breaking News

The Latest...

Results

The Results Are In!

Result Tally

...test Results

Results

Final Outcome

Voters will choose again on the next Election Day.

Voting is an important **right**.

CHILD

It is important for people to exercise their **right** to vote. Voting gives people the power to choose who will make decisions that affect their lives.

ADULT

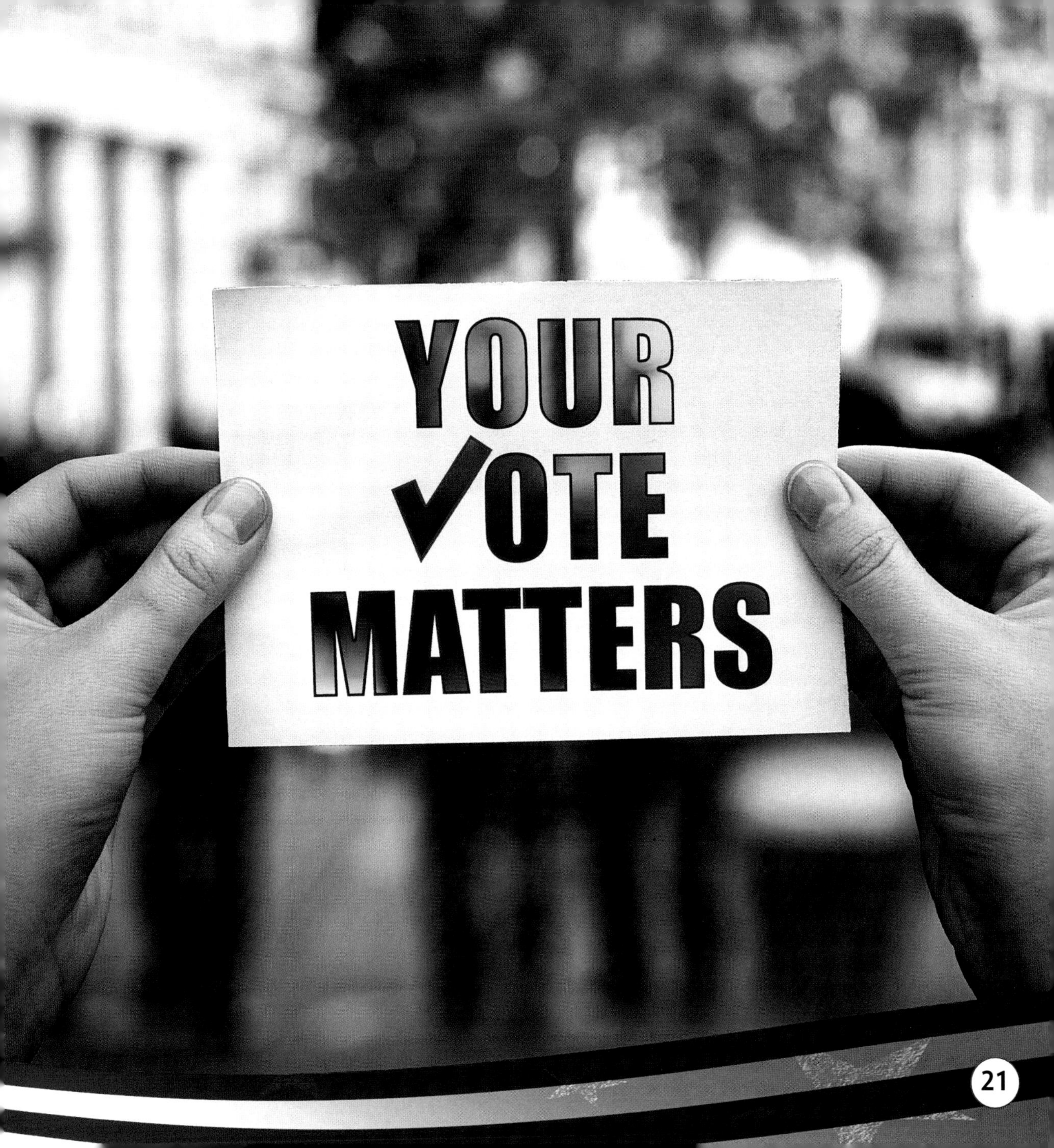
YOUR
VOTE
MATTERS

Words to Know

ballot (BA-luht): a form where people mark their vote

choice (choys): the act of picking one out of a group

citizens (SIH-tuh-zens): people who are members of a country and have the rights of that country

polling place (POH-ling playc): the building where people go to vote

president (PREZ-uh-dent): the head of the government in some countries, such as the United States

right (rite): something a person is allowed to do under the law

vote (voht): to make a choice for or against someone or something

Index

Comprehension Questions

1. When do people vote for leaders?
   a. on St. Patrick's Day
   b. on Thanksgiving Day
   c. on Election Day

2. Everyone must make their voting choice on a _____.
   a. website
   b. cellphone
   c. ballot

3. A polling place can be
   a. a library.
   b. a school.
   c. both A and B.

4. **True or False:** Voting can be done through the mail.

5. **True or False:** Voters must be at least 21 years old.

Written by: Tracy Vonder Brink and Madison Parker
Design by: Kathy Walsh
Editor: Kim Thompson

Library of Congress PCN Data
We Read About the Right to Vote / Tracy Vonder Brink and Madison Parker
I Read! You Read!
ISBN 979-8-8873-5199-5 (hard cover)
ISBN 979-8-8873-5219-0 (paperback)
ISBN 979-8-8873-5239-8 (EPUB)
ISBN 979-8-8873-5259-6 (eBook)
Library of Congress Control Number: 2022945528

Printed in the United States of America.

Photographs/Shutterstock: Cover © Orlowski Designs LLC,
©Lightspring, ©Vertes Edmond Mihai: Pg 4-21 ©Lightspring:
Pg 3 ©Monkey Business Images: Pg 5 ©Alexandru Nika: Pg
7 ©Minerva Studio: Pg 9 ©vesperstock: Pg 11 © Monkey
Business Images: Pg 13 ©The Toidi: Pg 15 ©Andrey_Popov:
Pg 17 ©Castleski: Pg 19 ©iQoncept: Pg 21 ©StunningArt

Seahorse Publishing Company

www.seahorsepub.com

Published in the United States
Seahorse Publishing
PO Box 771325
Coral Springs, FL 33077